The Great Life Mindset

By

Roy A. Piercy

The Roy A. Piercy Group

Quotes by Jim Rohn, America's Foremost Business Philosopher, reprinted with permission from Jim Rohn International ©2016. As a world-renowned author and success expert, Jim Rohn touched millions of lives during his 46-year career as a motivational speaker and messenger of positive life change. For more information on Jim and his popular personal achievement resources or to subscribe to the weekly Jim Rohn Newsletter, visit www.JimRohn.com.

The Roy A. Piercy Group

Paperback ISBN: 978-0-578-17941-4
Hardback ISBN: 978-0-578-17945-2

PRINTED IN THE UNITED STATES OF AMERICA

Book Dedication

Who to dedicate this book to was an easy decision. I am no-where the person I was 23 years ago when I met this lady!

It has taken five years to write this book. I wrote it in my spare time while running my dental laboratory business. Judy listened to me talk about this book and put up with me as I was trying to finish it. She never complained as I kept moving self-imposed deadlines and was supportive through the whole process.

So Judy, I dedicate this book to you. The one who is a major factor in making my life complete. With love, Roy.

Acknowledgements

In life, being around different people has a major impact on how your life turns out. I have been fortunate to have been around individuals, friends, professionals, and family who have been a positive influence and have helped me become who I am today. I am so grateful for their friendship, advice, and for being wonderful examples.

I want to thank my precious wife, Judy, who stands with me, supports me and makes me whole.

I want to thank my wonderful young adult sons and daughter, Ryan, Craig, and Amy along with Tara, Monica, and Michael. My grandchildren are Chelsei, Ethan, and Caleb.

I'm so thankful for the parents whose principles helped shape me into who I am today: my mother, Bonnie I. Gartsu, my stepfather, James D. Gartsu, and my father, Roy O. Piercy.

I have been a dental technician for 35 years and I have seven doctors that not only have been great clients, but even greater friends and practically family to me: Dr. Donald W. Ambler, Dr. Michael D. Caporal, Dr. Luis L. Dancausse, Dr. Lloyd M. Johnston, Dr. Patrick J. Kelley, Dr. Brian P. McNulty, and Dr. Craig C. Stoner. I thank you for all you have done!

I wish to thank and acknowledge three individuals whose programs and lectures I have listened to countless times. These were a real blessing and motivation in my life. I know one of them personally. They are Bill Staton, Jim Rohn, and Robert Allen.

I would like to thank Angie M. Fisher and Outskirts Press for all their work in making this into the product you see today!

Table of Contents

*"The greatest thing in this world
is not so much where we are,
but what direction we are moving."*

*Oliver Wendall Holmes
1809 – 1894 age 85
Physician, Poet,
Professor, Lecturer,
and Author*

*"Gaining knowledge
is the first step to
wisdom.*

*Sharing it
is the first step to
humanity."*

—Unknown

About This Book

I wrote this book because I have something to share. Something that can and will make a difference in other people's lives! If everybody kept great thoughts to themselves, we wouldn't have all the inventions that you see today. Just think about it for a moment. The way we live and the modern conveniences we enjoy today are the result of someone having an idea, having learned something from it, and having shared it with others.

As I have gotten older and wiser, things I did not understand earlier in life are clear to me now. Like many, I have learned things the hard way. I often needed a 2x4 board to hit me on the head to learn something, or had to have things come to a crisis point before I took action. I have made my share of mistakes. One thing about mistakes is that although everybody makes mistakes, it is what you learn from them that matters. To me, the worst and saddest thing of all is if you make a mistake and do not learn from it! Worst still, you doom yourself the possibility of repeating it.

My intent in this book is to make a genius out of you! What do I mean by this you may ask? There is a saying that a genius is someone who learns from other people's mistakes. This is what I hope for you. In this book I will tell you about my experiences, what I have been through, and how these experiences will benefit you! You have the opportunity to learn from my mistakes so you don't do them yourself.

I have named this book the "Great Life Mindset" because

if you apply the various mindsets that I will be outlining, you will enjoy a more fulfilling, happier life. The first half of this book deals with the attitude of your finances and covers the basic purchases that most people make in their lifetimes. We will talk about income, credit history, and the purchase of houses and cars. The second half of this book deals with personal development: your philosophy, your attitudes towards what you value in life, your character, what makes you tick, and who you are. I'm not saying you have to apply all of them, or do like I do, but I hope I can offer some thoughts or ideas that could have a huge impact on your life! How many times have you heard someone say, "Boy, if I could go back in time, I would have done this or I would have done that!" We all have choices in life and the choices we make now will have an impact on us down the road.

The main benefit you gain from reading this book is that if you do not have your priorities in order, it will give you incentive to get them in order. I see so many people out there who have problems that really are not problems at all. They just have misplaced priorities. A lot of people get upset over the dumbest things! Most times it is not the problem, but the perception of the problem. The common denominator is the person in the mirror.

If everybody threw all their problems in a pile and you were able to see the problems other people have, you might just reach in and take yours back!

In this book, you will see many common mistakes people make in their finances, their thought processes, and why they act or react the way they do. Much of what I will be going over isn't taught on a regular basis, if at all!

So I want to say thank you for purchasing this book. I pray that it will bring meaning, a little education, and make a positive difference in your life!

Sincerely,

Roy A. Piercy

Mission Statement

To make a positive
difference
in other people's lives.

To help people
look at life in a
totally different way
than what has been
considered the norm.

Introduction

Hello, I'm Roy A. Piercy. First of all, I want to thank you for purchasing this book! I hope that the knowledge and benefit that you gain as you read will be worth thousands of times more than what you paid!

One thing you will learn about me is that I'm pretty no-nonsense. In other words, I'm one of those that just tells it like it is. I'll probably step on a few toes or hit home with some of you, but it's for your own good!

What I'm trying to do is give you simple, easy-to-understand principles that will give you a good foundation so that you'll know what to do when obstacles that come your way. Answering any question is easy if you know the answer! The basis is this: I don't want you getting at the end of your life and realize that you've only lived 20% of it! You spent 80% paying for mistakes you made during the 20%! You might have blown valuable time watching too much TV, making terrible financial decisions, or having a terrible philosophy.

I give credit where credit is due and acknowledging those from whom I've learned and received information. I'm certainly not going to take credit for someone else's work. As a matter of fact, I want you to be able to look up the teachers and speakers who I've learned from so that you can further the knowledge that I'm trying to share with you.

You will see a lot of my favorite quotes as you read, as well as who wrote them. Under their names I put into a few words what they did, along with their birth and death year (if they are deceased) with their age. I do this because I want you to realize that some of them did not live to an old age. I do this to point out that you are not guaranteed to live to an old age either. So whatever you want to accomplish in life, my only advice is GET WITH IT! When you accomplish different goals and plans in your life, make it fun and reward yourself for accomplishing them! I hope you enjoy reading this book!

Thanks again!

Roy

CHAPTER I

Making Your Milkshake

Understanding Your Money

I have some good news for most of you folks out there and it has absolutely nothing to do with me or this book.

If you make $25,000 a year or more in a forty-year standard working lifetime, you will have over a **million dollars** go right through your hands. If you make the median household income of $50,502 as of 2014, that means over **two million** will go through your hands! Isn't that great news! Now for the bad news. Most Americans will **spend it all!** They will arrive at sixty-five years of age with nothing to show for it. Do you know what the new model of retirement is for this generation? NO RETIREMENT! In 1983, sixty percent of Americans had some kind of defined benefit (pension) plan. Today, 2015, it is less than twenty percent. Most Americans will rely on Social Security as their main source of income in their retirement years.

I don't want you to be in this category as you live your life. As a matter of fact, I don't want you even considering Social Security in your long-term plan. Here is my thought on Social Security or (So-So Security). Yes, I feel it will always be around. However, Social Security is to run out of money in 2037, if not sooner. Once this happens, two things are sure to happen. Benefits will dramatically be reduced, and cost will dramatically go up!

Keep in mind, money is not the most important thing in life. But make no mistake, money is important! You will either manage your money, or your money will manage you!

Money in itself is not good or bad. It has a current, that's why they call it currency. There are good and bad ways to acquire it. You certainly want to be in the good part. But let's get real, we go to school to get an education to do what? To have an opportunity to be able to do what you want in life and earn an income while you're at it. Most of the time, people focus on the income part and end up with jobs they didn't have in mind, or that weren't their passion. According to recent studies, eighty-five percent of the American public are going to jobs they hate or to a job that does not challenge them! If this is you, start figuring out what it is you want to do and go for it! You only have one life to live. You can't go back and start over! I'm sure I'll repeat this a time or two before the end of this book. Your life will go by faster than you can imagine.

> *"You will either manage your money, or your money will manage you!"*

So let's start off with the way to look at money. Money is the means by which we exchange the value of one item for another. You can't go into a grocery store and exchange a box of nails worth fifteen dollars for fifteen dollars' worth of groceries. That's not going to happen! Everyone in business wants money for their services and that's just the way it is.

Mindset on Your Income

Here is what you need to understand about your income. Your income is based on your value in the marketplace. You may say that you are worth fifteen dollars an hour because that is what you're paid per hour when you're working on your job. You can't say you're worth fifteen dollars an hour for the simple reason that when you're not working, you're not making fifteen dollars an hour! If you were worth fifteen dollars an hour, you could just stay at home and let them send you your money. You would wake up richer than when you went to bed. The bottom line is that you are paid fifteen dollars an hour for the labor that you do in an hour because that is your value to the one you're working for. To combat this, however, we want to create a situation during your working years so you can be worth that amount of money and more whether you are working or not!

Let's Make a Milkshake

Think of your income as if you were making a milkshake. The more income you bring in, the bigger your milkshake. Right now, your main income may be what you earn on your job. This is called linear income, the milk part of the milk-shake. As you go on with your working life, you want to cre-ate other forms of income, just like the syrup, flavoring that you add to make your shake. Other forms of income can be dividends from owning stock, or interest you earn on sav-ings, or royalties from an invention, or from direct marketing, or a money-making hobby. You may not be this far along. If you are not, you need to get busy figuring out what you can do to have other means of income other than your job or profession.

Now, maybe your job or profession pays a great salary or high income! If it does, here is my next question. Do you save any of it? You would be surprised as to how many don't! Most folks do not manage their money very well. Seventy-seven percent of families in this great country of ours live paycheck-to-paycheck. You hear of people you thought were rich being in the news filing bankruptcy. You hear of highly paid athletes, professional players, doctors, lawyers, companies, and corporations going bankrupt. How does this happen? The answer is not complicated. As a matter of fact, it's simple! They did not have good control of their money. They were not good stewards of it! Bad habits were practiced over and over until a day of reckoning ar-rived. These folks all had one thing in common, they all lived above their means!

We are in an earn and spend society. We are an instant gratification group that buys on impulse, not realizing the long-term consequences of our actions. We have the atti-tude that something <u>greater</u> is going to happen to us <u>later</u>!

Most Americans work hard! Most are well-meaning and

> *"Seventy- seven percent of working people in this great country live paycheck to paycheck."*

good people. The news pays attention to the 1 percent that are bad. Every time you hear of a crime that is so bad, you think it couldn't get worse, along comes one that is worse. Getting back to the good, today's society is so focused on teaching us to learn a profession so we can work for money; it doesn't teach us to have money work for us! We work ourselves to the bone during our working years and when those years are over, we end up broke and wondering what happened! This is the mindset we have to change. How much money have you saved in the last five years?

If you haven't saved any, who sold you on that plan? I suggest you do not do that during the next five! We need to have money work for us while we are in our working years. If a person would just sit down, put the cell phone on silent, leave the TV off and just think things through. Think of where you're headed. We're not a bunch of stupid people, but due to not thinking, we do stupid things!

Many of our Moms and Dads can't teach you about money because they hadn't learned themselves. How can they teach you something they don't know? We are a credit-based society and this is what most of us have been taught. In the next chapter, we will go over that credit-based society and how it gets entangled in our day-to-day lives.

Getting back to that milkshake, all the forms of income you come up with make up that milkshake! The main thing I want to say to you about money is that it doesn't matter how much you make; it matters how much you keep!

The Mindset of Money

Things Money Can Buy		Things Money Can't Buy
House	....	Home
Companion	....	Friend
Bed	....	Good Night's Sleep
Health Insurance	....	Good Health
Good Time	....	Peace of Mind
A Place in this World	....	A Place in Heaven
Lover	....	Soulmate
Laughter	....	Happiness

The Mindset of Money

❖ Whether we admit it or not, money dictates our moods. When money is low, we get stressed and our attitudes suffer.

❖ 90 percent of all divorces had money as one of the problems in the marriage.

❖ A dollar that you spend is gone forever.

❖ 25% of all purchases are unplanned.

❖ A dollar that you save is always around and then some.

❖ It's easy in this country to earn a lot of money but it's hard to accumulate wealth and become financially independent.

❖ You're in the richest country in the world! There is no reason you should end up in poverty.

❖ If a lot of money is your priority in life, you'll never be happy because you'll never have enough.

❖ Money is just a tool used to trade one value for another. Always look at it this way.

❖ Money is not the most important thing in life. However, it is important. Don't make light of it, but keep in the right priority.

❖ Money just makes you more of what you already are. If you're a giving person, it entitles you to give more. If you are a heavy drinker, it'll help you become a drunk.

WHO'S DRINKING <u>YOUR</u> MILKSHAKE?

CHAPTER 2

Who is Drinking Your Milkshake?

Part One
Mindset of the Credit Card

Now that you have figured out what it takes to build your milkshake, let me introduce you to the suckers out there that want to get their straws into your milkshake. They're like snakes in the grass! They spend millions of dollars advertising, getting your attention to go down the path of the world of credit. They don't get together at roundtables, but their purpose is the same. That purpose is getting every dollar out of you that they can. They are what I call the credit industry. The four majors that affect the most people are mortgage, car, student loan, and credit card companies. The mortgage and car industries are so big that they have their own chapter in this book. So right now, I'll address the credit card industry, and student loans.

First of all, I'm going to make it perfectly clear that I'm anti-debt. Why, because I know what living and depending on credit can do to an individual. It all starts out well-meaning and good intentioned. You get out of school, work hard and in comes that pre-approved hard rectangle thing in the mail. You start using it and at first you're purchasing small amounts of stuff and paying on time. Because of that, they keep raising your limit and you keep paying, and the limits go higher and higher. Then, you start buying more expensive items with your card. All of a sudden, you're not paying that card off in full every month and you are now introduced to that new word on your statement called interest. There goes the trap, smack, and you stepped right into it. Now you're a debtor, and a straw that doesn't belong to you (but in there because of your actions), gets inserted into your milkshake. That straw is not there for looks, it's sucking on your milkshake!

"The worst thing you can financially do to yourself is saddle yourself in a lot of debt."

You may think to yourself, that's not going to happen to me. Sad to say, poor use of credit is the third leading cause of bankruptcy in the U.S., with credit card debt being the main factor. The average credit card debt, according to CreditCards.com, is $5,596 per adult that carries a card. This is astoundingly high. The average individual in

2013 seeking Chapter 7 bankruptcy protection has around six credit cards with an average debt of $23,300! All this started with a little at a time and built itself up through bad spending habits.

It's happened to me, and yes, I have been bankrupt. I used to think credit was the eighth wonder of the world. I used to think that this was the way it was supposed to go. I thought the more cards, the more of a successful I was becoming. I deserved them. At one time, I had about twelve cards and some of the limits were in the $25,000 + range.

So you can probably guess what eventually happens when you have that kind of credit laying there. Sooner or later, something is going to happen that you tap it. These banks and issuers of credit cards know this. That's why they give you higher and higher limits. They're waiting for you to step your foot in that trap. It's only a matter of time.

> *"Never use credit cards for credit. Pay in full each month. No exceptions."*

So through experience, I know what I'm talking about! Been there, done that and it's not a place you want to visit! I want you to learn from my mistakes and please listen to what I have to say. Never use credit cards for credit! If you cannot pay the credit card bill you receive in full upon receipt, cut the cards up and pay the bill off! Nip this in the bud! Failure to pay your credit card in full each month is the first red flag that you're headed for trouble down the road. One of the mindsets in this book is to keep you out of debt so you can save money. Servicing credit card debt will keep you from forming good saving habits, so don't let this happen.

So now you're probably going to say that you need credit cards to build a credit history. Not necessarily so, but since I'm preaching about having no debt whatsoever, I have only one exception that I would only use credit cards for as far as building a credit history.

Okay, here is the only guidelines that I would follow as to using credit cards to build a credit history.

1. Have not more than 2 credit cards no matter your income, 1 VISA, 1 MASTERCARD, NO OTHER TYPES example: gas, department stores, retail.
2. Have a low limit on them so you could pay them IN FULL each month. No more than $2,000 - $3,000 tops! If they automatically raise your limit, just don't use it.
3. Do not charge more that 25% - 30% of your card credit limit. Example: On a $2,000 limit issued card, never go over $600 on the card. Make that your personal credit limit. Reason: Charging more than that will hurt your score and defeat the purpose of having them.
4. Only use the card for items you were going to buy anyway. Example: gas for your car. Buy nothing else with that card! Example: Travel – security purposes.

The only reason to build a good credit history is so that you can be in a position to buy a house. After purchasing a house, I wouldn't have any credit cards whatsoever! Use debit cards after the purchase of your home. The debit card you use for personal use, make sure to keep that account with a low limit. In other words, a card for use often, such as for eating out, movies, shopping at department stores, etc., keep a low limit in case your identity is compromised. Don't let the bad guys have a big payday at your expense. I'm sure you've heard of people's credit card numbers being stolen from department store databases: Target, for example. Sure, you have certain protections with your card, but it's a hassle.

Mindset of the Credit Card

- ❖ Never use credit card(s) to get credit (loan.)
- ❖ Pay balance in full upon receipt, don't wait on due date, no exceptions
- ❖ Don't use or obtain low quality cards such as those for department stores, gas, or specialty shops, etc.
- ❖ Studies show that you spend more with credit cards than with cash.
- ❖ You're tempted and usually buy more stuff than with cash.
- ❖ You'll pay more for the same stuff with credit cards because you're less concerned about prices.
- ❖ You're less aware of how much you've spent. (An average of 30% more at grocery stores.) When McDonalds accepted credit cards in 2004, they averaged $7.00 per card customer compared to $4.50 for a cash customer.
- ❖ 60% of cardholders do not pay their full balance

every month! (The banks smile!)

❖ 78% of people surveyed said they would borrow on a credit card if an emergency ever came up. (Why? They have no emergency fund and they are living paycheck to paycheck.)

❖ 96% of people who receive a credit card do not read the attached credit card agreement.

❖ Credit cards are fee heavy. Fees charged by credit card companies on statements include:
- Late fee
- Insufficient funds fee
- Convenience check fee
- Over-limit fee
- Annual fee
- Statement fee
- Phone fee
- Activation fee
- Inactivity fee
- Membership fee
- Services fee

❖ No such thing as easy payment. Have you ever found making payments on stuff easy? Just one of the falsehoods those in the credit card industry uses.

❖ Never give your credit card number over the phone unless you are the one who placed the call.

In 2002, about 3 million borrowers aged 50 and older carried $42 Billion in student debt.

By 2012, about 6.8 million debtors age 50 and older carried $155 Billion.

More than half of borrowers age 75 and up are in default on Federal Student Loans compared to 15% under age 50.

It gets worse. If you have Federal Student Loans and default, your social security benefits can and will be garnished.

Source: AARP Bulletin/ Real Possibilities December 2014

CHAPTER 2

Whose Drinking Your Milkshake?

Part Two
Mindset of the Student Loan

This is an area that is becoming a nightmare for many students. I'm not going to make light of an education. An education is important and will always stay with you, but how you handle your education and how you pay for it is important as well! Thirty percent of all college students that have student loans drop out of college. So, this is my thought on that statistic, if and when you decide to go to college, you need to have a clear direction and know what you want to do in life! Unless you are certain, I would not take out a student loan to begin with. Why in the world do you want to saddle yourself with debt with no direction? Let me give you some other statistics to help bring this to light.

"30% of all college students that take out student loans are dropping out of college".

Washington Post article
5-29-12

One Harvard study found that only 56 percent of students who enter four-year programs graduate within six years, while only 29% of those who enter two-year programs completed their degree in three years. Americans complete college at lower rates than poorer countries tracked by the Organization for Economic Cooperation and Development (OECD). The OECD tracked 18 countries and guess who finished last of the eighteen? You got it, the U.S. 46% of American students completed college once they started. A few of the countries we're behind are Japan with 89 percent, Slovakia at 63 percent and even Poland at 61 percent.

The cost of an education in the U.S. has sextupled since 1985 and student loan debt passed $1 trillion in 2011. Twenty-five percent of people with student loan debt are behind on their payments. This is just for regular non-profit colleges and universities.

At for-profit colleges and universities, the problem is even worse! More than 75% of students at for-profit institutions fail to earn a degree after six years! The for-profit institutions I'm talking about are the ones you see advertising on TV with regularity.

All colleges and universities whether profit or non-profit will work with you on student loans. Why? Not for the reason you think! They have a vested interest into making money for the institution they work for! The business part of the education process is at the forefront.

The student loan program, while well-intended, is like having another mortgage. With penalties and interest, dollars add up and before you know it, your balances can far exceed the amount you borrowed.

If you go this route for your education, make sure there is a demand for your services. It would be very expensive for you to have gone through two to six years of college, only to find there is no demand for your hard work. So think carefully about the major you choose. It's not about getting the degree anymore.

A college education is a privilege and not a given right.

First of all, let's put the mindset of a college education in the right perspective. If you decide to go to college to further your education, it is a privilege and not a given right.

Secondly, it is not up to your parents to send or pay for your college. If you believe that, you have been misguided, it's your responsibility, a part of your growing up and being an adult. If you have parents who have been good stewards of their money and have saved for your college, you are very fortunate, financially speaking. What you need to do if this is the case, is to be very diligent to make sure those dollars are used wisely.

We are in a culture today that doesn't have much patience. As a result, there is no real planning or real thought to our actions. We have

> *"A college education is a privilege, not a given right."*

a buy now and pay later attitude that has come with grave consequences. This chapter should help you develop a mindset that changes your attitude about paying for your college so that by the time you graduate, you have little or better yet, no debt when you walk down the aisle at graduation to receive your degree.

A true story that tears at my heart (and should yours), a grandmother several years ago co-signed a student loan for her granddaughter, who was pursuing a master's degree.

When her granddaughter couldn't find a job in her field of expertise after she graduated, she failed to keep up with the payments on the student loan the grandmother had co-signed for. Guess who the lenders went after to make good on the $60,000 debt? You got it, the grandmother!

The grandmother (age 77) is now forking over $415 a month or 15% of her social security along with money from a pension. To add insult to injury, she is working part-time to pay down the loan also.

I ask, as a grandson or granddaughter, would you do this to your grandparent? I certainly wouldn't even consider it! Here's another, I wouldn't do that to my parents either! Your parents raised you to adulthood; don't put them on the hook for your loans.

What avenues should you do in planning for college

expenses? Exhaust yourself applying for scholarships and grants. Let good old <u>work</u> come into play. Attend a community college for a few years and get some of the basic required subjects out of the way.

Depending on what field or career you're going after, you may just need to go to a trade school. Not everybody is cut out for college. It depends on your situation. Just think it through carefully before you decide!

I realize that I have been very negative in this chapter when it comes to college. College can be very rewarding to those who have a purpose and passion for what they want to do in life! Don't get me wrong here, but I have to point out to those who are thinking of taking student loans without a passion or purpose in this chapter to consider how high the stakes are if things don't work out. A high school graduate with a purpose and passion will outdo a college grad with no purpose or passion and have a more fulfilled life!

> *"A 77 year old grandmother is forking over $415 a month to pay on a student loan she co-signed with her granddaughter. Not good on any day!*

Mindset of College

1. What do I really want to do with my life?
2. Do I want to take on massive debt to accomplish this!
3. It is my responsibility to pay for college and no one else's
4. Is there a demand in the field I am pursuing?
5. Is this my passion?
6. 35% of college students drop out their first year.
7. 43% of students who start college don't finish.
8. By average, a college graduate makes about $1 million more than a high school graduate over the course of a lifetime. However, that doesn't mean that they get the most of it due to how they handle it.

Mindset of Debt
The Most Common Financial
Mistakes People Make

1. <u>Excessive/Frivolous Spending:</u> Buying things you don't really need.
2. <u>Never Ending Payments:</u> Financing everything you buy. Cars, furniture, appliances, you name it!
3. <u>Living on Borrowed Money:</u> Credit cards, long mortgages, payday lending.
4. <u>Buying a New Car:</u> Keeping a lifetime of payments going every time you purchase.
5. <u>Buying Too Much House:</u> Buying more house than you need. Rooms you don't even use. Sooner or later you'll fill it up with stuff you don't use.
6. <u>Treating Home Equity Like a Piggy Bank:</u> You dip in and suck the equity out of your house, usually on things you don't need.
7. <u>Living Paycheck to Paycheck:</u> You just joined 77% of the U.S. population. You spend it as fast as you get it. In many cases, faster.

"It is my hope that by recognizing mistakes and by being aware of them you may avoid making them yourself."

8. **<u>Live Below Your Means!</u>**

Source: Staff of Investopedia followed by the author's comments.

"Never judge a person by the car they are driving. They may be up to their neck in debt trying to impress you, and everyone else. A car does not make the person! It is a depreciating form of transportation. Just because one is driving an expensive car, doesn't mean they are richer and well to do!"

Roy A. Piercy

CHAPTER 3

Mindset of the Car

Best Ways to Buy a Car

Financially, the first six chapters of this book are important. But this chapter is one that you should pay close attention to. Outside a house purchase with a mortgage, the automobile is the main purchase of all Americans. Purchased in the wrong ways, this can also be the costliest of all the purchases you make. In this chapter, I will be giving you some facts as to what people are doing to purchase cars and some of the predicaments they get themselves into. Hopefully, you're not one of those who fall into the stats that I will reveal in the following pages! Once you're done with this chapter, you will be more aware of what to look out for so you're not trapped or tricked into a purchase that is not in your best interest.

We are a culture that wants to have the best car now! If the payment fits, we buy! Let's say an individual goes to a car lot and buys a brand new car with a loan (which 70.5% of car buyers do!). The moment he or she drives that car off the lot, the car has depreciated 10 – 15%!

> *Fact: 70.5% of people finance their cars. 18.5% lease. Only 11% pay up front with cash.*

There are savers and investors who would love receiving 10 to 15% on their investments in a year's time and a new car owner will squander that much in 1 minute! That new car that you thought was a new car is now considered a used car! How about that? Doesn't that just want to make you stop a minute and let that sink in? Think that through for a moment. That new car feeling is going to last about a month. That is until that first payment is due. Then it's a payment each month for the next five, six, or seven years depending on the deal. The most popular at the time of this writing is six years or 72 months. Seventy-two months sure is a long time to make payments on something that is going down in value. Something else to consider here is, can you reasonably predict what your job, or health circumstances are going to be in six years? All it takes is for something to happen for a three-month period or an accumulation of three months and you can be in a mess. If you get in financial trouble, I promise you they will repossess that vehicle! Do not kid yourself or think you are a special case. The very day a payment is 90 days past due, an order will go out for repossession; you will find out who the <u>real</u> <u>owner</u> is when that happens!

Getting back to that new car, what is scary to me and should be to you is that one third or 30% of people who get a new car that they are financing are upside down on the car they are trading in. What I mean is that they still owe money on the vehicle they are currently driving that they're using as part of the deal! When this is taking place, you have given advantage to the dealer or lender in the negotiating process! It's called a rollover and what one owes in debt is added to the new car price. You open yourself up to having to pay more for a vehicle, which is already more than it's worth, and you will pay a higher interest rate due to the increased risk on the lenders part. When you look at all the vehicles on the road in the U.S. that's a lot of vehicles that are upside down! If your rollover is more than 10% of the purchase price, this is a dangerous predicament to be in. Why? Because you will be upside down for a longer period of time in your new vehicle!

With the average price of a new vehicle at $33,560, according to Kelley Blue Book researchers, that's a lot of money being laid out on the table. That's money you could be saving for your benefit instead of giving it to the lenders and car companies. Don't let those fancy showrooms fool you when you walk into them and the light is bouncing off those shiny cars or trucks right into your eyes! That's to blind you into what can be a major purchasing mistake. Dave Ramsey says that "the worst car wrecks take place on the showroom floor." I totally agree, for while you're gazing at a vehicle, a salesman will be right there to make you feel like you're entitled to that vehicle. He or she is going to get you to picture yourself driving it! That's why they readily hand over the keys so you can go test drive so you can get those emotions rolling. You thought they gave it to you so you could see how the vehicle handled. I've never test driven a new car that handled bad. If you think about it, depending on your age, you haven't either! So the main reason for test driving that new car or truck is to play on your emotions and get you to buy!

I cannot begin to list all the types of deals that car dealers can throw at you because of all the variables. One thing I can say is that if you're not one of the fortunate few who can pay cash they will structure a loan to meet what you think you can afford in payments. The dealers have all kinds of ways and means such as adjusting the interest rate, extending the term of the loan, which in turn can add thousands to the total cost of the vehicle.

Now, some of the scariest and I mean scary stories I have been told and actually seen, is that a lot of folks are buying high priced cars and getting eight and nine-year loans! One went out and bought a $60,000 car with a home equity loan! Remember that interest-eating-money shredder I told you about in another chapter! I have to use exclamation marks here for I hear of this happening and all I can do is shake my head.

As far as advertising goes, the dealers take up 95% of the commercials during the evening local news, at least where I live. One evening, I counted the different car commercials during a 30-minute period. I kid you not; there were 22 commercials just on cars and trucks. All that is just getting you to their showroom floor at their dealership. So the dealers are spending huge amounts of money on advertising and you already know the reason. I'm now going to share a story with you of three individuals who each had $4,000 in their hand to go buy a car. Since the average car payment at this moment is $509.11, all three had $509.11 a month in their budgets to pay for a car. In the meantime, car A, B, and C rolled off the assembly line one after the other. In other words, the exact vehicle's make, model, etc. The only difference is that they were bought at different times. The amount of money used was the exact same for a four-year period.

Car A, Car B and Car C roll off the assembly line. They are 2010 models and are exactly the same and are priced at $32,400 each. Ryan buys Car A as a new car right from the dealership, while Amy and Craig buy Car B and Car C as used cars at later dates.

Ryan	Amy	Craig
$4,000	$4,000	$4,000
January of 2010	January of 2010	January of 2010
Ryan buys Car A with $4,000 down and finances $28,400 @ 8.8% for 72 months, payment is $509.11.	Amy buys "clunker" for $4,000 cash. Amy saves $509.11 per month.	Craig buys "clunker" for $4,000 cash. Craig saves $509.11 per month.
2 years later (2012) Ryan making those $509.11 payments, 48 payments to go. Car is worth $22,680.	2 years later (2012) Amy tires of clunker, trades in on Car B $2,000 trade-in +$12,218.64 cash $14,218.64.	2 years later (2012) Craig still driving clunker. Has saved $12,218.64.
	Amy buys Car B for $22,680, pays $14,218.64 and finances $8,41.36 for 24 months. payment is $375.01 and adds $131.10 to payment.	
4 years later (2014) January of 2014, Ryan making those $509.11 payments 24 payments to go. Car is worth $18,370. He still owes $12,218.64.	4 years later (2014) January of 2014, Amy has Car B paid in full in July of 2013. Amy saves $509.11 per month. January of 2014 has $2,545.55 in bank.	4 years later (2014) January of 2014, Craig decides to donate clunker to family who needs a car. Craig buys Car C for $18,370 cash! And has $6,067.28 in bank.
After 4 years, bought new ($12,218.64)	Bought 2 year old used +$2,545.55	Bought 4 year old used +$6,067.28

All 3 NOW HAVE THE SAME CAR!

Folks, do you notice what a little patience and good money management can do? In just four years time, Ryan who has bought the car new is still $12,218.64 in debt. Craig who bought the same car with cash has $6,067.28 in the bank (or invested). This is a difference of $18,285.92 for the same car with the same money! I don't know about you, but that's powerful! This is just a four-year period of time. Let me ask you this, What if you in either of these scenarios, did this for 30-40 years, or your lifetime? What a difference this could make in your life financially if you just changed your attitude toward an automobile and looked at it as a means of transportation instead of a status symbol. Whenever I look at someone in a new car, I mostly wonder if that person is in debt or if they paid cash and are they the real owner of that car. If you have a car with payments, you are not the real owner of that car. I'll take a paid-for used car in good working condition over a new car loaded with debt any day!

After reading this chapter and hopefully understanding it, can you see why so many Americans are in bad financial shape? Remember, this is one of the straws in your milkshake!

"A hundred years from now it may not matter what my bank account was, the sort of house I lived in, or the kind of car I drove...but the world may be different because I was important in the life of a child."

Forest E. Witcraft
1894-1972 age 72
Scholar, Teacher,
Boy Scout Executive

CHAPTER 4

Mindset of the House

Best Ways to Buy a House

When it comes to the word mortgage, John Commuta of the "Transforming Debt into Wealth" system describes it the best I ever heard. In Latin, the word mortgage means death grip. The words *mort* meaning death and *gage* meaning grip. So every time I see the word mortgage mentioned, I think death grip. Owning your own home is the so-called American Dream and I sure do want you owning your own home! I just want you doing it in ways that do not create a death-grip around your neck.

Don't strap yourself

Like everything else, there's a right way and wrong way of doing things. Purchasing a house should be a fun experience as much as possible. I have seen far too many young couples go purchase too-much-house and stress

> *"The word mortgage in Latin means death-grip."*

themselves out making the high payments. Like the car, they have that image thing going on. Nothing to me could be more frustrating than moving into a large high-priced house and not being able to do many of the simple things because you can't afford to. What fun is that?

You need at least 20% down

The best measuring stick and rule-of-thumb to go by in the down payment is do you have at least 20% down to put on the purchase price of the house? If you do not, that's your first red flag that you can't afford the house! You're also going to get stuck with PMI (private mortgage insurance) that will be added to your monthly payment. It's money that you've totally wasted. This insurance protects the lender at your expense! If something happens to you and you default, the lender is covered. You fall on your face; they don't care! I know that sounds a little hard-hearted, but it's the truth! Banks and other mortgage institutions are in the business of making as much money off you as they can. They come up with more schemes and underhanded tricks than you can imagine. They have more types of

> *"If you don't have 20% for a down payment, you can't afford the house!"*

mortgages than you can shake a stick at. They have different down payment products, different lengths of payments and so on. Their main objective is getting the highest rate of interest and payment they can get away with. The industry standard is the 30-year mortgage with interest calculated according to your credit score. Do you realize that in the first eight years of a 30-year mortgage, you have only paid just under 10% of the principle on the mortgage? Talking about putting money in an interest money-eating shredder! You still owe $150,018 on the original $176,000 on a $220,000 house. I do not want to see you in this category! On a 15-year mortgage, after eight years, you would already be over the halfway mark on your entire mortgage!

If you finance, insist on a 15-year mortgage, maximum

The difference of paying a 15-year mortgage and a 30-year mortgage payment is really not that much! Simple reason, the interest portion of your loan is so much larger on a 30-year mortgage. For example: on a $220,000 house at 4.5% with a mortgage payment of $866.00, the difference between a 30-year monthly payment and a 15-year monthly payment at 3.25% is only about $371.00 a month. Best deal of all, a 15-year mortgage is fully paid off in just 15 years!! Reward yourself with a bottle of champagne and a three-week vacation with that one! Just think what you can do with a paid off mortgage!

Please, oh please don't get a 30-year mortgage with the idea that you will make extra principle payments to pay it off in 15 years. I've heard that strategy more times than I can count! According to the FDIC, people using the plan end up not sticking to this plan a whopping 97% of the time. More events and reasons and excuses will come about that will keep you from doing that. If you can't make the payment on a 15-year mortgage as compared to a 30-year, make that your second red flag that maybe you can't afford the house.

Don't make a piggybank out of your house

One of the worst things you can do to yourself at any time during any phase of owning or paying on your home is to use your house as a piggybank! What do I mean? I'm talking about getting the so-called equity out of your house whether through refinancing and taking cash at closing or through a home equity line of credit, otherwise known as HELOC. It should be called HELL-LOC because that is where this loan comes from. Every time you refinance or dip into your home equity, you start the payment process at square one! If you're trying to pay a house off in fifteen years, (as you should), then you don't want to go down this path. So if this option is ever offered to you, just say no thanks!.

Best strategy for paying a house off early

Let's say you have an existing loan and have gotten a promotion by which you have a higher income. You are able to make extra principal payments each month easily. Instead of paying the extra principle payment to the lender, put that payment amount in an investment account until the balance in this account equals the balance of your mortgage. Once this occurs, pay off the mortgage! Why am I saying this? You need to keep in mind that you are helping the lenders security when making the extra payments at the risk of your own. If something went wrong, such as a job layoff or sickness, you could tap the money in an investment account. However, if you give the extra principle payment to the lender, and something goes wrong, the lender will foreclose the moment you stop making payments. Like I said before, the lenders don't care if you fall flat on your face or not! It's wonderful to pay your house off early, just do it with your security in mind and not the lenders. The banks and mortgage companies have already proven that by how they acted during the last housing bubble.

Do not look at your house as an investment

Your house is a place to live! You've got to live somewhere. Used to be you could buy a house and the values were always going up. But that logic has changed over the last fifteen years. The last housing crisis brought that to light. So don't have the thought that just because you purchase a house, its value will always go up. That's just not true.

Story of Brian and Luis

Brian and Luis work doing the same job making the same money. They happen to live in the same neighborhood and each bought basically the same type house. They paid $220,000 each for the house. They both put down 20% or $44,000 on their houses. However, Brian got a 30-year mortgage and Luis obtained a 15-year mortgage. Excluding taxes and closing costs, which would be about the same, let's crunch the numbers and see how this works out. Note: they each had the exact same money!

	Brian	Luis
Cost of House:	$220,000	$220,000
Length of Loan:	30 years	15 years
Down Payment:	$44,000	$44,000
Balance:	$176,000	$176,000
Interest Rate:	4.25%	3.25%
Monthly Payment: (Sept. 2015)	$865.81	$1,236.70
7 ½ years March 2023	Bal. $150,017.35 Interest $52,274 You're at 25% point in mortgage	Bal. $78,312 Interest $33,961 You're at halfway point in mortgage
15 years Sept. 2030	Bal. $115,029 Interest $94,939	Bal. $0 House paid for
30 years Sept 2045	Bal. $0 House paid for	Has been paid for 15 years' prior
Mortgage Dollars Invested	$0	Has been investing $1,236.70 a month For 15 years at 13% interest. Has $688,447.14 in account. (at 6.5% interest $378,664)

Source: Bankrate.com

Financial independence...

"The ability to live from the income of your own personal resources."

Jim Rohn

1930 - 2009 age 79
Entrepreneur, Author,
and Motivational Speaker

CHAPTER 5

Winning Financial Formula for Your Life

It's All About Percentages

Ok! Let's get into the mindset of what financial independence really is! It is real FREEDOM! We live in the richest country in the world. We have all kinds of freedoms that people in other countries simply don't have. So here we are in the land of the free with all these freedoms at our fingertips except one that we have to work at. That is financial freedom. If you can be financially free in the land of the free, then you have true freedom!

So you ask, how can any regular citizen in this wonderful country of ours be financially free! First of all, I want you to know that I have studied dozens of financial programs, read numerous books and magazines and listened to dozens of individuals on the subject of financial independence or becoming rich. I do not like using the word rich because it carries a stigma that automatically alienates people. When the word rich is used, people automatically think of movie stars, sports stars, corporate CEOs, etc. or a class of people that is not them. Many people have the unfortunate thought process that nothing good is going to happen to them anyhow! You'd be surprised how many times I've heard that. This is the thought process we have to get away from.

I am all about simple and easy to understand! I don't like taking simple things and making them complicated. I am about making things as fun as reasonably possible. So let's put this plan in an easy to understand format. What I'm about to tell you is the most financially important statement that I can make in this book! Here it is: 1. <u>Learn to live on 70% of your net income!</u> This is income after paying your taxes. We all know that two things are certain, death and taxes, so let's get taxes out of the way right off the bat! You will be doing some wonderful things with the other 30% that will be the foundation for your financial life. 2. <u>10% you set aside for giving.</u> Giving is one of the greatest things you can do for yourself and others. 3. <u>10% you set aside for yourself.</u> This is the part in which you save so you can invest. 4. <u>10% is for fun.</u> Like I've said, make this fun, because if you don't make this fun, you will not do it for long. We will now address each of these four points in detail.

> *"Learn to live on 70% of your net income!"*

1. <u>Learn to live on 70% of your net income.</u> The earlier in life you understand, it will be the easier to do. This is the area where all your living expenses come. So, some work and detailed planning will need to take place here. There are so many situations that we could not cover them in this basic book. But do careful financial planning. Notice I did not use the word budget. I do not like that word either. So do a good financial plan and adjust it when necessary.

2. <u>10% you set aside for giving.</u> The main purpose of this is that giving is living! Having a giving nature makes you a more caring human being. It keeps the sickness of greed from entering your heart. I'm not a bible scholar, but it is said in scripture that God loves a cheerful giver. So we need to not only give, but do it in a cheerful, loving manner. We are very blessed in this life and we need to share our blessing with others. Those who follow this simple plan tend to be even more blessed than those who do not.

3. <u>10% goes to savings, so you can invest.</u> You cannot build yourself towards financial freedom if you do not save and invest so you can have other streams of income coming into that milkshake I mention in Chapter 1. Financial planning is a must have. They are many things to invest in. I have some recommended reading at the end of this book from the experts in this area.

4. <u>10% is for fun.</u> Two things I want you to do in this category. One is that I want you to set aside money here for weekend outings and vacation. The other is forming a money-making hobby. That could be

making things to sell, doing network marketing, starting your own company to help with taxes and speeding up your savings to invest. Just to do.

Right this moment, you may have circumstances by which you can't get on this plan. My statement is, work on it so that you can. The sooner you get on it, the better. It's important! Why important, because there is one element that has to kick in. That is compound interest! Remember, you want to get to the point you want your money to work for you. Compound interest is one of those ways.

> *"If you never save money, so you can invest, you'll always be poor, financially speaking."*

The following is a chart that every high school student should understand before graduating. Understanding this chart is so powerful. I wish I had a second chance at this (along with everyone over the age of 18)!

Meet Ethan, Chelsei, and Caleb and the power of Compound Interest

Ethan had graduated high school and had a part-time job. He put $167 a month into a self-directed IRA, which is $2,000 a year. He did that systematically for eight years and stopped saving—deciding to spend the money elsewhere.

Chelsei had graduated at the same time Ethan did, but had other interests. However, at the end of eight years, she also saved $167 a month or $2,000 a year and kept saving until she was 65 years old.

Caleb realized he had better start saving since he was 36 and wasn't getting any younger. He had a good job and was able to contribute $4,000 a year to his IRA. He kept saving that amount until he was 65.

All three had invested wisely and made an average return of 13%. The following chart on the next page will demonstrate how their savings and compounding worked out.

Age	Ethan's Yearly Investment	Ethan's Balance	Chelsei's Yearly Investment	Chelsei's Balance	Caleb's Yearly Investment	Caleb's Balance
19	$2,000	$2,260	$0	$0	$0	$0
20	$2,000	$4,814	$0	$0	$0	$0
21	$2,000	$7,700	$0	$0	$0	$0
22	$2,000	$10,961	$0	$0	$0	$0
23	$2,000	$14,645	$0	$0	$0	$0
24	$2,000	$18,809	$0	$0	$0	$0
25	$2,000	$23,515	$0	$0	$0	$0
26	$2,000	$28,831	$0	$0	$0	$0
27	$0	$32,579	$2,000	$2,260	$0	$0
28	$0	$36,815	$2,000	$4,814	$0	$0
29	$0	$41,601	$2,000	$7,700	$0	$0
30	$0	$47,009	$2,000	$10,961	$0	$0
31	$0	$53,120	$2,000	$14,645	$0	$0
32	$0	$60,026	$2,000	$18,809	$0	$0
33	$0	$67,829	$2,000	$23,515	$0	$0
34	$0	$76,647	$2,000	$28,831	$0	$0
35	$0	$86,611	$2,000	$34,839	$0	$0
36	$0	$97,870	$2,000	$41,629	$4,000	$4,520
37	$0	$110,593	$2,000	$49,300	$4,000	$9,628
38	$0	$124,970	$2,000	$57,969	$4,000	$15,399
39	$0	$141,217	$2,000	$67,765	$4,000	$21,921
40	$0	$159,575	$2,000	$78,835	$4,000	$29,291
41	$0	$180,319	$2,000	$91,343	$4,000	$37,619
42	$0	$203,761	$2,000	$105,478	$4,000	$47,029
43	$0	$230,250	$2,000	$121,450	$4,000	$57,663
44	$0	$260,182	$2,000	$139,499	$4,000	$69,679
45	$0	$294,006	$2,000	$159,894	$4,000	$83,257
46	$0	$332,227	$2,000	$182,940	$4,000	$98,601
47	$0	$375,416	$2,000	$208,982	$4,000	$115,939
48	$0	$424,221	$2,000	$238,410	$4,000	$135,531
49	$0	$479,369	$2,000	$271,663	$4,000	$157,670
50	$0	$541,687	$2,000	$309,239	$4,000	$182,687
51	$0	$612,107	$2,000	$351,700	$4,000	$210,956
52	$0	$691,680	$2,000	$399,681	$4,000	$242,901
53	$0	$781,599	$2,000	$453,900	$4,000	$278,998
54	$0	$883,207	$2,000	$515,167	$4,000	$319,787
55	$0	$998,024	$2,000	$584,398	$4,000	$365,880
56	$0	$1,127,767	$2,000	$662,630	$4,000	$417,964
57	$0	$1,274,376	$2,000	$751,032	$4,000	$476,819
58	$0	$1,440,045	$2,000	$850,926	$4,000	$543,326
59	$0	$1,627,251	$2,000	$963,807	$4,000	$618,478
60	$0	$1,838,794	$2,000	$1,091,362	$4,000	$703,400
61	$0	$2,077,837	$2,000	$1,235,499	$4,000	$799,362
62	$0	$2,347,956	$2,000	$1,398,373	$4,000	$907,800
63	$0	$2,653,190	$2,000	$1,582,422	$4,000	$1,030,334
64	$0	$2,998,105	$2,000	$1,790,397	$4,000	$1,168,797
65	$0	$3,387,858	$2,000	$2,025,408	$4,000	$1,325,260
Total Investment	$16,000		$78,000		$120,000	

Ethan's total investment was $16,000

Chelsei's total investment was $78,000

Caleb's total investment was $120,000

All three ended up with great totals! But as you can see, even though Caleb invested more than Ethan and Chelsei, he never caught up with them. Caleb never caught up with Chelsei or Ethan, and Chelsei never caught up with Ethan. Point being, the earlier you start, the more you can accumulate!

"Compound interest is the eighth wonder of the world. He who understands it, earns it... he who doesn't... pays it!"

Albert Einstein
1879 – 1955 age 76
Theoretical Physicist

It's your Choice
It's your Plan
It's your Life

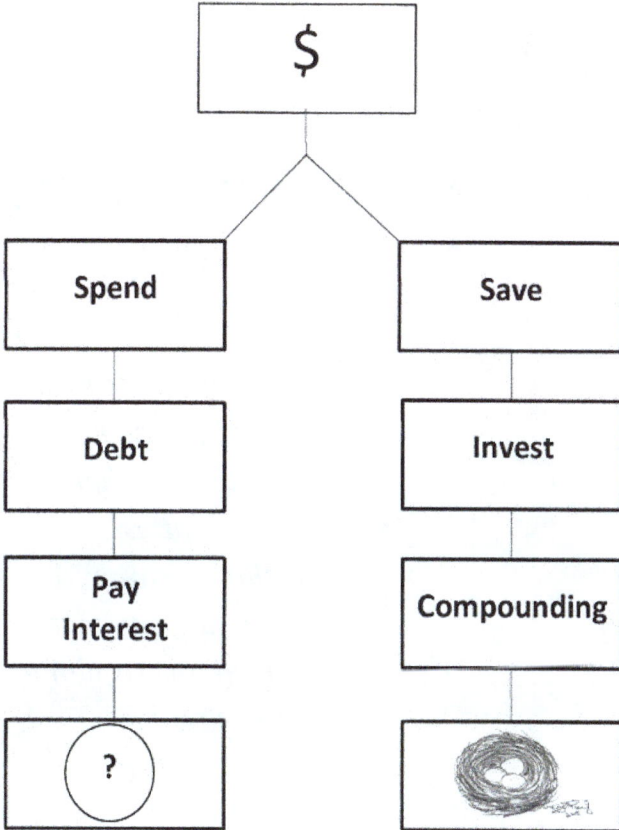

"Money makes money, and the money that money makes, makes more money!"

Benjamin Franklin
1706 -1790 age 84
Founding Father of the
United States
Author, Printer,
Politician, Inventor,
Statesman, Diplomat,
Politician

Financial Independence Mindsets

- ❖ Learn to live on 70% of your after-tax income.
- ❖ Set aside 10% for giving.
- ❖ Set aside 10% for yourself to invest.
- ❖ Set aside 10% for fun.
- ❖ Come up with an income-producing hobby.
- ❖ Compound interest works while you are sleeping.
- ❖ Timing is everything when it comes to compounding. The sooner you start, the better.

Be an optimist
and not a pessimist

"An optimist sees the rose
and not its thorns.
The pessimist stares at
the thorns, oblivious of
the rose."

Kahill Gilbran
1883 – 1931
Artist, Poet, and Writer

CHAPTER 6

Habits of the Richer and Habits of the Poorer

The Haves and Have-nots

In this chapter I'm using the words richer and poorer. Like I've said before, the words rich and the word poor have bad stigmas. It's like the rich are one group, the poor are one group, and then there's the in-between. Here, I'm talking of two groups all-inclusive. A lot of people are not poorer because of hard luck, and a lot of richer people are not richer just due to good fortune. There are reasons why there are two directions. It's habits, lifestyle, principles, values, and attitudes that make all the difference in the world.

I'm going to just take the following chart just to point out what I mean:

Habits

The Richer	The Poorer
❖ Invest money first and pay bills on what's left.	❖ Spend money and invest if there is anything left.
❖ Make plans and plan ahead whether it be financial, vacation, purchases.	❖ Don't make plans and just take things as they come. Maybe a vacation.
❖ Look to become financially independent by saving and investing.	❖ Will never achieve financial independence by spending everything they make.
❖ Tithe – about 3% of believers in the population do.	❖ 97% do not tithe
❖ Have a fund for emergencies and have it ready right now.	❖ Most people over 65 cannot write a $600 check on a moment's notice.
❖ Prepay on their mortgage (2.7%)	❖ Do not prepay on the mortgage (97.3%)
❖ Purchase used cars cash	❖ Finance cars every time
❖ Don't procrastinate, get things done in a timely manner	❖ Put things off, never seem to get things done
❖ Benefit from compounding interest	❖ Continually pay interest
❖ Have more assets than liabilities	❖ Have more liabilities than assets
❖ Know exactly where money goes	❖ "Don't know where it all goes"
❖ Do not play blame game. Look at problems as opportunities	❖ Blame everything on something else but themselves
❖ Read books and even have a library room in their house	❖ Read very little or hardly at all
❖ Will knock on a thousand doors to sell a product	❖ Will knock on a few doors and see what happens
❖ Figure out the system and works the system	❖ Try to beat the system
❖ Make themselves known to the manager of the bank	❖ Know only the tellers
❖ Buy items with cash or debit card or if with credit card, pay bill upon arrival	❖ Rely on credit cards and use as credit and pay ongoing finance charges

So you can see that people are not richer or poorer by chance, it's just due to their habits whether good or bad. It just goes to show that you can be sincere, work hard, and wind up broke.

The Rich and the Poor of the Bible

Proverbs 22:1   A good name is more desirable than great riches; to be esteemed is better than silver or gold.

Proverbs 22:2   Rich and poor have this in common: The Lord is the Maker of them all.

Not good to make yourself rich in the wrong way. Proverbs 21:6 says, "A fortune made by a lying tongue is a floating vapor and a deadly snare."

Proverbs 21:13   If a man shuts his ears to the cry of the poor, he too will cry out and not be answered.

Proverbs 21:17   He who loves pleasure will become poor; whoever loves wine and oil will never be rich.

Proverbs 22:7   The rich rule over the poor, and the borrower is servant to the lender.

Proverbs 22:9   A generous man will himself be blessed, for he stores his food with the poor.

Proverbs 22:16   He who oppresses the poor to increase his wealth and he who gives gifts to the rich – both come to poverty.

Proverbs 22:22   Do not exploit the poor because they are poor and do not crush the needy in court, for the Lord will take up their case and will plunder those who plunder them.

Proverbs 23:4,5   Do not wear yourself out to get rich: have wisdom to show restraint. Can't beat a glance at riches, and they are gone, for they will surely sprout wings and fly off to the sky like an eagle.

"The bitterest tears shed over graves are for words left unsaid and deeds left undone."

Harriet Beecher Stowe
1811-1896 age 85
Author:
Uncle Tom's Cabin

CHAPTER 7

Your Philosophy

Who are you?

Where are you headed in life? I have to ask this question because as I observe people in day-to-day life, I find that most are going through a usual work day with nothing on their mind but that magic 5:00 to come so they can just go home. They get home, get some dinner, watch TV a while, and go to bed. Next thing it's morning, go to work! That cycle repeats itself all week until the weekend. Even worse, many are working six days a week without much of a weekend at all! Before you know it, it's Sunday night and you get that sinking feeling because tomorrow is a workday and it's back to work mode. Does this sound like you? What if you do this day-in and day-out for five, ten, fifteen years? Do you get what I am saying? Nothing will change for you.

Many people go through life day-in and day-out without any direction at all! The great Zig Ziglar calls these folks wandering

> *"How many times have you heard someone say: "Someday I'm gonna do this or I'm gonna do that?" and never do."*

generalities. Many will never get around to what they were going to do some day. How many times have you heard someone say, "Some day I'm going to do this or I'm going to do that," but they never do?

Have you ever watched the TV show "The Pickers"? The series was about two individuals, Frank and Mike, who tour the country looking for antiques to buy and resell. It's amazing what people hoard and store for years and years. Many episodes have the same scenario, there'll be an old man who is walking with a cane in their late 70s or 80s, and have four or more buildings full of stuff. Frank or Mike will try to buy, for example, a motor to a motorcycle. Many times they come to a deal, but not always. A lot of times they can't come to a deal because they are going to do something with it some day! You look at their physical condition and you know it's just not going to happen!

Many of us will go straight to our graves with our songs still in us! I am into the Piercy genealogy and I have spent a lot of time in

> *"Many of us will go straight to the grave with our songs still in us."*
>
> *Zig Ziglar*

cemeteries looking for my ancestors' graves. I have the most fun doing it. I have gone into thick, wooded areas way out in the country, cow pastures, you name it. There is something out there for everybody. Next time you are at a large cemetery, look out over the landscape and think of what happened to those that are there. I know that's not the most pleasant thing to think about, but bear with me. Some died of tragic accidents, some of incurable diseases, some were victims of crime, and some deaths were a result of drug addiction, alcoholism, suicide, heart attacks and cancer and so on. Last, of course, many died of old age as their time had naturally run out. In a mortal world, you would hope that most had died of the latter, but sadly most are laid to rest before their time or before their life expectancy was up! One thing is certain, life on this earth is not guaranteed and unfortunate things happen to us that are out of our control! None of us can do anything about that, but let's get real, that is the exception and not the rule!

Another thing is certain, as you get older, time seems to go by faster and maybe it is. I heard in a sermon recently, to take plenty of pictures when you are in your twenties, for you will never look that good again! For in your thirties, your hair will turn grayer and your teeth will start hurting. In our forties, that hair and teeth start coming out or has to be tended to. In your fifties, places start hurting in your body that you didn't know existed. You start to become a regular in a doctor appointment book instead of a friend's address book. You will try to have lifts, tucks, and pulls done in an effort to return to the shape you were in in your twenties and thirties. I hate to be the one to tell you, but it's not going to happen!

So you might as well not worry about it. Oh, did I forget to mention, worrying will put you in an early grave also.

Ok, enough of the doom and gloom. It's not that bad! I was just throwing a little humor into the aging process. I've seen people in their forties and fifties in better shape than those in their twenties and thirties. Their secret is that they take good care of themselves and we'll touch on that later in this book.

So let's get back to the question, who are you? Are you someone with direction? Do you know where you are headed with your life? Do you know what you want to accomplish? Do you feel that you are in a rat race all the time? Keep in mind that if you win the rat race, that will make you the #1 rat! In life, the way we live our daily lives makes it easy for us to lose contact with who we really are. We get tangled up with what's going on in the world and forget what it is in life we were trying to accomplish.

So, sometime, take a good look at yourself and decide who you are! Decide on who you want to be. Only you can do it! Decide on who you are and who you are not! Decide on what people you are going to hang with. Remember, those you hang with will

> *"You can't soar with Eagles and hang with Turkeys!"*

certainly be an influence to how you turn out. I go by the saying you can't soar with eagles and hang with turkeys. So my suggestion is, be careful with whom you associate with on a constant basis.

Who Are You Mindsets

- ❖ I am somebody!
- ❖ I am in control of me. I will unselfishly control what goes on around me and how I'll spend my time.
- ❖ I am open to new ideas, starting with the reading of this book.
- ❖ I am going to look at life differently than 97% of the population in this country.
- ❖ God put me here for a reason.
- ❖ I am going to have a positive attitude and do away with negative thoughts because I have no time for them.
- ❖ I will decide what I want to accomplish in life and will set goals to succeed.
- ❖ It's never too late to be who I want to be.
- ❖ I will take 100% responsibility for my life by not making excuses and blaming others.
- ❖ My past will not control my future.
- ❖ Who you are, not what you do, is important.

"Don't be afraid to give your best to what are seemingly small jobs. Every time you conquer one, it makes you stronger. If you do the little jobs well, the big ones will tend to take care of themselves."

Dale Carnegie
1888-1955 age 66

CHAPTER 8

Quality, Attitude, and Commitment

Doing Your Best

The very important aspects of your life that come into play here are quality, attitude, and commitment. Funny how your way of thinking can have such an impact on how your life turns out! Experiences that happen to you early in your life have an effect on you today, whether minor or major. I'm going to tell you a story about something that happened to me in my senior year of high school that got my attention when it came to quality, attitude, and commitment.

When I started my senior year of high school, I had a fairly easy schedule, for I had taken most of my required courses in the previous years. But one subject that I had put on my schedule was a course known as Math Concepts. Like all students, I was strong in many subjects and not so strong in others. Advanced math was not one of them! To get into Math Concepts, my previous year's Algebra II teacher had to sign off in order for me to get into the class. My Algebra II teacher, Mr. Hamilton, said he enjoyed having me in his class that year, but I was going to have a hard time in Math Concepts and felt I should not do it. He said he would sign off, but I was in for a hard time. My thought at the time was, *I'll show you*, and I made the commitment that I'd study hard and prove to him and myself that I could handle it!

Well, we all listen to our teachers, right? I started taking Math Concepts and I studied, and studied and the more I tried to get it, the less I understood. I was having a hard time and getting frustrated just like Mr. Hamilton said.

My homeroom teacher that senior year was the same I'd had my junior year, Mrs. Knox. She was a very dedicated teacher, the type you were comfortable being around, one you could really talk to. So I let her know what a pickle I had

> *"The greatest discovery of my generation is that a human can alter his life by altering his attitudes."*
>
> *William James*
>
> *Educator, Psychologist, Author*

gotten myself into and that my GPA was going to suffer if I didn't do something. She let me know that she needed one more student in her Home Economics class that period to meet the minimum amount of students she needed to teach the class.

I thought, Home Economics! Are you kidding? That's for ladies! I can't be seen dead in there! She said yes and if I was willing to do that, she would get me out of Math Concepts. With that got-ya smile she said, "the choice is yours." I looked at her and said "okay" and found myself in a Home Economics class full of ladies, but there was one other guy in there who had the same look in his face the first time I saw him. I thought to myself, oh hell, how did I get myself in this mess! My attitude was to keep a low profile and just get through it.

The first project that we were able to do was making a dress jacket or sport coat, complete with lining. My thought was that I would just do it and just get it done and move on. My first assignment on this project was to go get the material for this jacket we were going to make. So I went to this fabric shop and purchased the cheapest material on the bargain table. It was a scarlet material with a burgundy design on it. It looked awful! I just didn't care and when Mrs. Knox saw it, she had a surprised look on her face, but didn't say anything.

Mrs. Knox was a tall, 6'2" African American lady. You could tell she liked the job she was doing and she was easy to learn from. I learned how to sew on the sewing machine and was surprised as to how well I was doing on the jacket. When it was finished, the workmanship was wonderful! I couldn't believe it! But then there was that awful fabric that I bought at the bargain table in the fabric store.

Mrs. Knox told me that I would've had a nice sports jacket to wear if I had just taken my time and selected some decent fabric. She was right and I promised myself that no matter how minor the task, I would do all phases to the best of my ability. That one project changed my attitude. It changed my philosophy, and in that moment changed my commitment. The following projects I did in that class with my new attitude, I aced. Outside of doing the usual cooking and household things that you do in a Home Economics class, I made a bookshelf and a dinner table, which I used for years afterward. I had a lot of fun in that class. At the end of the year on awards day, I received the outstanding student award for Home Economics. When the student body heard my name, instead of laughs, I was only one of a few students to receive a standing ovation!

> *"It's a very funny thing about life; if you refuse to accept anything but the best, you very often get it."*
>
> W. Somerset Maugham
>
> 1874 - 1965

I learned more from that class about quality, doing things right, having a positive attitude, and not worrying about what other people think than any other class in high school. I'll always be grateful to Mrs. Knox who made a positive difference in my life.

That class was the springboard for my new thought process in other classes as well! That wasn't the only out-standing student award I received that day! I got one for Architectural Drawing as well. Later, I got another in college in Dental Laboratory Technology.

Now when it comes to commitment, I think of three guys that work out at the YMCA where I go in the mornings when I can. These three guys, C.J., Sam, and Kerry, do an inten-sive weight lifting and go at it for an hour and twenty minutes six days a week! You can set your watch at 5 am for that's when they start. They are dedicated to what they do. They are very polite and no-nonsense type of guys. The result of their workouts? I nicknamed them the Hercules Brothers. They bench press in the 400-pound area, not bad for indi-viduals who just do it to keep in great shape. I don't expect you to do like they do, but I would hope you would develop a commitment to a great attitude and doing things to the best of your ability.

"Faith in Christ is voluntary. A person cannot be coerced, bribed, or tricked into trusting Jesus.
God will not force His way into your life.
The Holy Spirit will do everything possible to disturb you,
draw you, love you-
but finally it is your personal decision."

Billy Graham
1918 - Living age 97
Evangelist and Author

CHAPTER 9

The Greatest Life Mindset

One-on-One Relationship with God

As I have been writing this book, you have noticed that I've said that this chapter was important or that chapter was important. Sure, all the chapters in this book are important; however, this chapter is the most important! Friends, I am not going to beat around the bush here, but the most important thing you can do for yourself is to have a one-on-one relationship with God! Without that, the foundation for your life will be a sandy one! That's where the "On solid rock I stand," phrase comes from. Christ is that rock!

This is a basic edition and we're not going into a bunch of issues. Like I've said before, I don't have an agenda, except to help as many people as I can. I try to keep things simple and uncomplicated. With that in mind, it is my sincere hope that in your lifetime (if you haven't already), you should form a one-on-one relationship with God. It's all about you and the Heavenly Father. For doing so, God has a gift for you, and that's eternal life! It doesn't get any better than that! Jesus made this possible by dying on the Cross for everyone.

Personally, I received Christ on May 6, 1972 in the Charlotte Coliseum (now called Bojangles Coliseum), in a crusade conducted by the Rev. Billy Graham. Rev. Graham is now 97 years old as of this writing, and all but one of the quotes in this chapter is my personal tribute to him. I am so thankful for what he has done in my life and for the lives of others. Have I strayed from time to time? You bet!

I have had the privilege of going to many different churches through the years, all of them preached the gospel and focused on Christ. I've been in the Baptist, Methodist, Presbyterian, First Assemblies of God, and the Seventh-Day Adventist Churches. Do I agree with every single thing they all preach? I do not. I go by what the Bible is saying to me. I have a quote I keep in my Bible that I will share with you at the end of this chapter. All the churches I've mentioned above have the most wonderful people I've ever met attending them. I'm not going to tell you where or which one to go to, but make sure they're Bible-based and focus on God. Make sure they don't have some other agenda. Make sure you're being fulfilled and learning more about Christ. That's about as simple as I can be on the subject right now.

"There is no room for God's Word in our culture, where our children are without reverence for God or faith in the Bible. There is no room for our Lord's creed of purity and self-denial, when the media sends forth a constant barrage of profanity and indecency and materialism."

Billy Graham

Some things to be aware of in this day and age is as you watch the media. The amount of profanity and indecent behavior and materialism is increasing with each passing season. Things that would not have been allowed on radio and TV just twenty years ago are commonplace right now. If you're already aware of it, then you know what to look out for. If you're not aware, then the culture of it will creep into your mind and body and you will see nothing wrong with it! This is the deception that Satan has put into to the world for years. So get to know God, study His word, and pray every day. Whether it is on your knees, looking up at the sky, or talking as you go about your daily activity; He hears you! God is omnipresent, meaning He is everywhere. God has left the decision to us whether we want him in our lives or not.

"I have never been to the North Pole, and yet I believe there is a North Pole. How do I know? I know because somebody told me. I read about it in a history book, I saw a map in a geography book, and I believe the men who wrote those books. I accept it by faith." The Bible says, "Faith cometh by hearing, and hearing by the word of God" [Romans 10:17 KJV]

-Billy Graham

"*Going to church will not make you a Christian any more than sitting in a garage will make you a car.*"

Joyce Meyer
1943 – Living age 72
Bible Teacher,
Author and Speaker

What says the Bible?

What says the Bible?
The blessed Bible,
this my only question be?
The teachings of men,
so often mislead us.
What says the
Bible to me?

Franklin E. Belden
1858 – 1945
Author

Just a note to unbelievers:

"I would rather live my life as if there is a God, and die to find out there isn't, than to live my life as if there isn't, and die to find out there is!"

Anonymous

"In general, the shape of your body is the result of what you have been eating, whether good or bad. The healthy or unhealthy actions you have taken, or the exercise you have or have not done!"

Roy A. Piercy

CHAPTER 10

Health Chapter

Take Care of Yourself
Simple English on Your Health

This may be the shortest, simplest, to the point chapter in this book! Why, because only two words are needed: diet and exercise.

In a way, I hate to use the word diet because that word is so abused. While we're at it, the work exercise is abused just as much! When most hear the word diet they're thinking of types of diets. That is not what I'm talking about. I'm talking about the different foods we are eating. Heard the expression, you are what you eat? I believe this to be true. A lot of us are eating some of the unhealthiest junk foods and it's showing up on our waistlines in staggering numbers.

It's annoying to me that we Americans can spend hundreds of millions of dollars on fad diets, exercise equipment, and as a whole, we keep getting more obese, and get less exercise than ever before. Health and Physical Education has all but been kicked out of our schools.

As Americans, we love to eat! We are a land of plenty and we consume plenty as well. On average, we should not consume over 2,000 calories a day period. I was in one restaurant, which I will not write the name of because that's not my point, but they had a giant of a meal being offered. It was a burger with two, six-ounce beef patties with cheese, bacon, fried onion strips, tomatoes, and their spread sauce on the buns. Served with that was a large serving of steak fries with a large caramel milkshake. To say that I was a little curious as to what the calorie count on such a meal would be is an understatement. I researched it and found that one meal, just lunch, came to 3,540 calories. That's about two days' worth of calories. It had about 3 ½ days of saturated fat, along with 3,000 milligrams of sodium (between the burger and the fries), which is about two days' worth also. Now to the large shake, 38 teaspoons of sugar. Burning off the calories would take twelve hours of walking! In essence, anything you ate (healthy or not) would just be added calories and fat for 2 days! This is insane and yet I saw half a dozen people with that particular meal.

Thankfully, most do not eat that much, but many do eat smaller portions of that type of food: hamburgers, hot dogs, fries, pizza, pasta, etc.

Getting back to basics, fruits and vegetables should make up most of your diet. Nothing beats fresh vegetables and fresh fruits in season. Take advantage of that. I would go as far as saying two thirds! We are fortunate to be able to basically have plenty of fruits and vegetables year round depending on what it is of course.

An apple a day keeps the doctor away. How many times have you heard that? It's probably the most effective prescription ever given because it's true! Compared to other fruits and vegetables, apples have proven to be one of the most potent weapons against heart disease, cancer asthma and type II diabetes! Apples are full of super antioxidants. The antioxidant level active in just one apple is equivalent to 1,500 milligrams of Vitamin C, although it contains 5.7 milligrams. One important thing to keep in mind, eat the apple with the peel as opposed to without. Depending on the variety, the peel contains two to six times the antioxidant compounds than if you ate the apple peeled. My favorite is the Fuji, which contains the highest levels of antioxidant compounds. But, you can't go wrong with whatever variety. Please make them a part of your daily diet. There are also other benefits, so look them up and gather more information on apples. While you are at it, look at all the benefits of beans. Yes, beans! Beans are a wonderful source of potassium, magnesium, iron, B vitamins, fiber and low fat proteins! They're also loaded with phytonutrients, which are important antioxidants. When I say beans, I mean all beans,

> *"Apples have proven to be one of the most potent weapons against heart diseases, cancer, asthma and type II diabetes."*

peas, and lentils. The most popular being pinto, Great Northern, garbanzo, green, snap peas and green peas. I could eat my weight in lima beans.

Another great source for nutrients is the fruit in the berry category: blueberries, blackberries, strawberries, cherries, and so on. These are loaded with an-

> *"Beans are a wonderful source of Potassium, Magnesium, Iron, B-vitamins, fiber, and low-fat proteins."*

tioxidants as well. I haven't even covered the vegetables such as greens, tomatoes, onions, cucumbers, squash, and melons. I could write a whole book on fruits and vegetables, so I believe you get the point I'm trying to make as far as your health is concerned.

When it comes to meats, there are a few basic rules I go by. As far as beef goes, I'm all-in on grass-fed beef! It's much healthier than grain-fed beef. Do some research on that and you will be amazed at the difference! With poultry, whether chicken or turkey, you can taste the difference between organic and grain-fed birds. I'll go organic on that.

When it comes to fish, the fish caught in the wild are best in my opinion. My main reason is that the wild fish eat more natural organisms like zooplankton, which is a rich source of omega-3 fatty acids. The main benefit of omega-3 fatty acids is that they've been proven to increase your good (HDL) cholesterol, reduce blood pressure, and stabilize your heartbeat. In addition, omega-3 acts as a blood thinner. Another important benefit is that omega-3 fatty acid may play a role in preventing breast and colon cancer!

However, due to over fishing and pollution, you're going to have to do your homework on the fish you are eating. Atlantic salmon are almost extinct, so most are farm-raised. Swordfish, shark, king mackerel and tilefish are loaded with mercury, so I avoid these altogether. My favorites are haddock, tilapia, Alaskan whitefish, halibut, and flounder. As of now, these are testing low in mercury. I'm not the best connoisseur of other types of seafood, but research what you're eating when it comes to seafood. You have a good idea when it comes to your diet, so eat healthy!

Exercise

The basic on exercise is this. Get moving! One in three Americans over the age of 50 does not exercise at all! The danger in not exercising is that your body loses 25 to 35% of muscle mass, which results in loss of strength, and an overall decline in your physical being. With all the modern conveniences we have at our disposal, we are moving less than past generations.

Right now the typical American burns around 300 calories a day, but consumes around 2,100 calories. You don't need to be a math major to figure out that imbalance. When you look at all the chronic diseases in our culture, the main underlying culprit is the food we eat and lack of physical activity or exercise! Though genetics may affect some people no matter what they do, that is the exception and not the rule.

I have heard some people say that genetics is why they're in bad shape and can't exercise, but it's a lousy excuse and they're covering up being lazy. That might sound mean but it is what it is! One thing I can promise you, if you get some physical activity, even if it's walking around the block one day and two blocks the next, you will feel better after you do it. And yes, walking is exercise! On the next page, I will list the benefits of exercising and you can decide for yourself. These are proven facts and in some cases, common sense.

> *"When you look at all the chronic diseases in our culture, the underlying culprit are the foods we eat and lack of physical activity."*

Some direction comes straight from the Bible. It says in Corinthians 6, verses 19 and 20: "Do you not know that your body is a temple of the Holy Spirit, who is in you, when you have received from God? You are not your own; you were bought at a price. Therefore, honor God with your body." Whoa! Isn't that some good information?

So, if you are already exercising, that's great. Keep it up! Most people find that once they start exercising, they see and feel the results and continue to do it. They make it part of their lifestyle. It's not a fad; it's a lifestyle! It should be a part of one's daily life. Remember, your own heart is a muscle, therefore exercise it to make and keep it strong. That's one muscle you do not want declining! One of my favorite all-time speakers, Jim Rohn, says: "Take care of your body, it's the only place you have to live! It just can't be said better than that! Time is the most valuable thing you have and the only way you can have more time is to take care of yourself!

> *"Take care of your body. It's the only place you have to live!"*
>
> *Jim Rohn*

So, if you are not exercising, please start, and today is a great time to get going! What to do and when to start you may ask? The best advice I have heard and started doing myself was 30 minutes of walking daily. I have it tweaked to walking a mile every 15 minutes and built it up to running a tenth of a mile for every ½ mile of walking. You do what works for you and you'll know what works once you've started. So please, get started and make it as fun as you can!

Mindset of Exercise

Benefits of Exercise

❖ Makes your heart stronger.

❖ Burns calories to help you maintain a healthy weight.

❖ Helps control blood sugar to help prevent or manage diabetes.

❖ Increases your ability to concentrate and helps with alertness.

❖ Boosts the immune system to fight off disease.

❖ Will make your bones stronger.

❖ Proven to increase your level of endorphins, which are brain chemicals that increase your sense of well-being, improve your mood and fight depression.

❖ Helps reduce macular degeneration associated with cataracts.

❖ Increases metabolism to help burn more calories.

❖ Can decrease levels of LDL or (bad) cholesterol and increase the levels of HDL or (good) cholesterol.

❖ Helps the blood flow to the brain, which in turn helps with mental capacities.

❖ Reduces the risk of many diseases.

❖ Improves sleep.

❖ Gives you more energy.

❖ Keeps you young by delaying the aging process.

Mindset of Exercise

Exercise has Proven to Improve or Even Prevent

- ❖ Heart disease
- ❖ Stroke
- ❖ Coronary artery disease
- ❖ Colon cancer
- ❖ Breast cancer
- ❖ Prostate cancer
- ❖ Endometrial cancer
- ❖ Osteoporosis
- ❖ Obesity
- ❖ Disability
- ❖ Arthritis
- ❖ Dementia
- ❖ Chronic lung disease
- ❖ Type II diabetes
- ❖ Cataracts and macular degeneration
- ❖ Depression
- ❖ Sore butt due to sitting on it too much!
- ❖ Dizziness

To have purpose
that is worthwhile,
and is steadily being
accomplished.
That is one of the secrets
of life
that is worth living."

Herbert Casson
1869-1951 age 82
Canadian Journalist,
Author

CHAPTER 11

Design Your Life

Purpose

Have you ever seen the phrase, "Today is the first day of the rest of your life."? Have you ever sat back and let that sink in? Well, yesterday is gone and here we are today! Is today just going to be a continuation of what you were doing yesterday? What if you keep doing that another 10 years, where will you be? To you that may be fine, but I am suggesting that you take a good look!

<u>Time</u> One thing I can say is, time is so precious. As you get older, it does fly by. It seems like time has speeded up. So whatever you're wanting to do in life, I say, get with it!

Randy Pausch was an American professor of computer science at Carnegie Melton University. He gives a wonderful lecture titled, *Really Achieving your Childhood Dreams*. It was called "The Last Lecture," but they renamed it. At the time he gave this lecture, he had three to six months of good

> *"Time is all you have. And you may find one day that you have less than you think.*
>
> *Randy Pausch*
> *1960 – 2008 age 47*

health left. His lecture is on YouTube and I recommend you watch it sometime. Even though he knew he had little time left, he gave it all he had. On July 25, 2008, it was announced on Good Morning America that he had passed earlier that morning. My point here is that this could happen to us and at any time. That's why procrastination is such an enemy of fulfillment. Remember those old fellows I told you about on the TV program "The Pickers"? The guys can hardly walk, but will not sell an old car part or even an old car because they're going to do something with it someday!

Many folks out there have a low opinion of themselves. So in turn, they don't motivate themselves. Some have the attitude that nothing good is going to happen to them anyhow. I remember the movie "Moonstruck" where Cher slaps a man in the face and says, "Snap out of it!" So go in front of the mirror and do that to yourself if that is what it takes.

Change

If you keep doing what you've always done, you'll keep getting what you've always got! A lot can be said for those words of wisdom. If we keep our regular habits, nothing will change. So one of the most important actions anyone can

> "Beginning today, treat everyone as if they were going to be dead by midnight. Extend to them all the care, kindness, and understanding you can muster, and do it with no thought of any reward.   Your life will never be the same again."
>
> Og Mandino
> 1923 – 1996 age 72

take is to change. Og Mandino has a quote that I love and goes as follows, "Beginning today, treat everyone as if they were going to be dead by midnight. Extend to them all the care, kindness, and understanding you can muster, and do it with no thought of reward. Your life will never be the same again!" So how you treat people around you would be a great start to your change process if it's needed in that particular area. If how you treat people is not a problem, then take a look around and see what areas of your life do need changing. If you don't like where you are living, change it! If you don't like your job, change it! I realize you can't do all of this overnight, but start today! Jim Rohn says, "You can't change your destination overnight, but you can change your direction overnight!"

As far as your job goes, the most important recommendation I can make is that you find your passion. Something that you love to do. Figure out what it is you're good at. Everyone has God-given talents that sets them apart from others. You have to figure that out and go with it. Don't base this on money. If you do, you might miss the whole point of

> *"You can't change your destination overnight, but you can change your direction overnight."*
>
> *Jim Rohn*
> *1930 – 2009 age 79*
> *Entrepreneur, author, speaker*

finding your passion. I'm a strong believer that if you find your passion, the money will follow.

To me, I believe there are four areas that you can design your life around. I believe that if you excel in the areas I'm about to discuss, you will have a wonderful, fulfilling life. I'm going to list them and make a brief comment on each one and why.

Having a wonderful mate

I've always felt that was half the secret to success! Many of you reading this book are probably already there. Before Eve, Adam was in the garden of Eden and had everything at his fingertips, but he was lonely. Everybody wants to love somebody

> *"A man is never poor if he (or she) has friends.*
>
> *Jimmy Stewart*
> *1908 – 1997 age 89*
> *actor*

and be loved. Along with a wonderful mate, your family and friends fall in this area. If you don't have a mate right now, your family and friends fill most of that void. Jimmy Stewart said, "A man is never poor if he (or she) has friends." Your family almost goes without saying. Nothing is more satisfying than watching our kids and grandkids grow up and making a positive difference in their lives.

Being healthy and fit

If you don't have your health, you cannot enjoy life to its fullest. We are a funny bunch; we abuse our bodies trying to get wealth and then have to spend our wealth trying to regain our health! All we needed to do was to watch what we ate and moderately exercise. It's just that simple. So if you are healthy and fit, then you feel better than a lot of people out there!

Being financially independent

Talk about freedom! If you are financially free in the freest country in the world, how great would that be: being able to do things when you want to do them; getting up in the morning when you want to instead of an alarm waking you up out of your sleep. There is a lot to be said for these things. Working because you want to instead of because you have to, there is a big difference there. Being able to help others and being able to afford to help others is so satisfying and rewarding!

Having a one-on-one relationship with God

I'm not a great Bible scholar and I'm not a religious freak, and I'm not asking that you buy into what I believe. But I do believe we were created and I've covered in Chapter 9 the basics of what I do believe. This is not a religious book, and I have no agenda going on. If you don't have a relationship with God, all I suggest is that you give it some attention, for it'll be a positive, life-changing experience! I truly feel that if you have these four principles going for you, you'll be happier and more at peace than 99.9% of the people on this planet!

Relationship with Your Spouse

❖ Tell her or him you love them at least once a day, for that will never get old.

❖ Never go to bed angry with your spouse. Discuss and take care of whatever the problem is before going to sleep or else you won't get quality sleep and prolong the hurting. And never sleep apart!

❖ It's not only in marrying the right person; it's being the right partner.

❖ Never too old to hold hands.

❖ Making each other better people.

❖ Having common values and objectives.

❖ Being united when it comes to dealing with your children if you have any.

❖ Husbands, open the door for your wife and help with her coat!

❖ Time with your kids is priceless. No time spent with them is ever wasted.

❖ Never miss the chance to dance with your spouse. I always think of that song from Lee Ann Womack.

❖ Be quick to give praise to your spouse when they do great things.

❖ Be quick to say I'm sorry when you're in the wrong.

❖ Never say anything uncomplementary about your spouse in the presence of others.

❖ In disagreements with your spouse, never bring up the past. Deal with the situation that's happening now!

❖ Always tell your spouse how terrific they look.

❖ Don't be critical and say negative things about your spouse's friends. A long lasting relationship is like a new day. You start all over again in the morning!

*A person once said to
Helen Keller:
"It must be sad not to
have your sight."
She replied,
"No, but what is sad
is to have your sight
and have no vision!"*

*Helen Keller
1880 – 1968 age 87
Author, Political
Activist, Lecturer
First deaf-blind person to
earn a Bachelor of
Arts Degree*

Mindsets of Keys to Designing Your Life

❖ **Believe in yourself!**
If you don't believe in yourself, no one else is going to believe in you either.

❖ **Work on yourself!**
Work hard on yourself to make your life have the greatest sense of purpose possible. Make yourself a better person.

❖ **Figure out what it is you're living for!**
Are you living to make things better for you and those around you?

❖ **Passion.**
Do you have passion about what you do? Do you have a sense of pride, or ownership in what you do? If money wasn't an issue, would you do what you do for free!

❖ **Problem solver.**
Can you take problems that come your way and look at them as opportunities to conquer?

❖ **Can you plan?**
A lot of frustration can be eliminated if we plan things instead of just letting things happen. What things would you like to accomplish?
"A goal without a plan is just a wish." – Antone De Saint-Exupery

❖ **Are you service-minded?**
One of the greatest secrets of success is serving others. The more you serve others, the more you will receive in return.

"Working hard is not enough. Your rewards will always match your level of service." –Earl Nightingale

❖ **Do you have great relationships with those around you?**

I'm not only talking only about your spouse and your children; I'm talking about everyone around you and those you associate with. We live in a society connected through social media. What you put in emails and social media is going to reflect on who you are, especially to strangers.

❖ **Do you have great ethics and values?**

Are you honest and trustworthy in all that you do?

❖ **Do you have goals?**

What things do you want to accomplish? What are you about? What you *get* by achieving your goals is not as important as what you *become* by achieving your goals.

❖ **Do you want to leave a legacy?**

Did you make a difference in other people's lives by being here?

❖ **Do you want to be a success?**

Whether I'm a success or not will not be determined by me or other people. The success I want is determined by God himself.

George Herbert Walker Bush, our:

41st President of the United States
43rd Vice President of the United States
11th Director of the CIA
Chief of US Liaison to China 1974 – 1973
10th UN Ambassador 1971 – 1973
US House of Representatives 1961 -1971
BA from Yale University
US Navy 1942 – 1945

was asked what his greatest accomplishment was?

This was his answer:

"My kids still come home to see me!"

Funny how life goes

When I was a kid,
I was dying to get to high school
When in high school I was dying to get my driver's license
Then I was dying to turn 18 and become legal
Then I was dying to graduate and start college
Then I was dying to become 21 and be legal drinking age
Then I was dying to finish college and start my career
Then I was dying to buy a house, get married and start a family
Then I was dying for the kids to grow up and get in a position to retire
Now that I'm retired and dying I realize I forgot to live!
Author unknown
Don't let this be you!

Be thankful for wherever you are in life currently and enjoy each day!

Life is short, folks! You can live life anyway you want to but you can only live It once. You can't go back and start over.

Learn not to have a silly ego, be quick to forgive, believe slowly, love truly, laugh often, and never avoid things that make you smile!

"Do you really want to be happy?
You can begin by being appreciative of who you are and what you've got."

Benjamin Hoff
1946-Living
Author

CHAPTER 12

Keys to a Happy Life

Gratefulness

Have you ever been around someone who has a negative attitude all the time? Not for long, I'll be glad to tell you that! I can't stand it and will not listen to it for a period of time. Why? Nothing good will ever come from it. I am convinced that some people wouldn't know happiness if it kicked them in the rear end. I decided long ago that I don't have time for it and neither should you!

Life involves choices. It is you who decides how your life is going to go. Life is what you make it! I know you have heard that before and it's true. Just like Charles Kaurault would say, "What lies around the bend?"

Below I have some principles I go by that have made a difference in my life and can give you food for thought in yours.

*Have a forgiving nature Studies show that those who

have a forgiving nature have better lives than those who hold grudges. Example: The Hatfields and McCoys, a feud that lasted from 1863 to 1891. At the end, four Hatfields, one sheriff's deputy, and seven McCoys were all killed. That's the extreme, but I've seen family members be so begrudged that they wouldn't speak to one another all the way to the grave (How sad.)

*Love yourself and what you stand for Love yourself, but don't be in love with yourself, that's selfishness. If you don't like or love yourself, how do you expect others to like you? Make other people around you happy and you'll be happy. Lighten up. You've heard the saying: live well, love much, laugh often. Laughter is one of the most natural medicines to make us feel great!

> *"We tend to forget that happiness doesn't come as a result of something we don't have, but rather of recognizing and appreciating what we do have."*
>
> *Frederick Koenig*
> *(1774 – 1833) age 58*
> *Inventor, a partner of*
> *Speed printing press.*

*Don't procrastinate Procrastination is one of the worst enemies in life. Putting off until tomorrow what you could do today only leads to frustration later!

Be happy with what you have So many people drive themselves crazy wanting something else. They are never fulfilled. Frederick Koenig said it best, "We tend to forget that happiness doesn't come as a result of something we don't have, but rather from recognizing and appreciating what we do have."

Be thankful for everyday! I'm in my late fifties now! I can say that with an exclamation point because about 23 years ago, something happened that almost killed me. What I'm about to say, I haven't discussed with anyone, not even my wonderful wife until this writing. I felt that I needed to share this story in the hopes that if anyone out there is feeling hopeless, they'll read this and feel otherwise! If the story I'm about to tell makes a difference in just one person's life, then it's worth telling.

It was a rainy night and I was sitting at my work desk in my laboratory. The wind was blowing hard and the rain was splatting against the glass windows. It was two o'clock in the morning, and I had tears running down my face. I just couldn't stop it. I was staring right at bankruptcy. The realization that all I had tried to accomplish was amounting to zero was more than I could take. I felt like such a loser and failure. I had recently been granted a divorce from my first wife of 17 years. At the time of my first marriage, I had promised myself that I would never even consider a divorce, let alone get one. I'm not going to get into details about the divorce except to point out that I had broken a promise I had made to myself. I felt so worthless!

Anytime you look back on life, you can see where rock bottom was in your life, and for me, that night was rock bottom. I had accumulated a lot of things in that time period. I had two houses, two office buildings, a mountaintop property, a wonderful business and all of it was crumbling down.

As I was sitting there at my desk, I thought, "How in the world am I going to be able to show my face to anyone! I'm a loser, a failure, and a sorry, useless human being. I knew that I could take my 357 and erase everything! I could end all this misery and not have to feel this anymore. I picked up my gun and had it cocked, I put it to my head, and then, bam, I froze. I was ready to squeeze the trigger when my eyes caught a little picture of my two sons that I had sitting on my desk. **IT WAS AT THAT MOMENT THAT EVERYTHING CHANGED IN MY LIFE.**

This picture helped save my life

The first thought was, "How could you be so sorry as to leave your sons to fend for themselves and leave your ex hanging like that? The least you could do is to provide for them until they can provide for themselves. At that moment I laid the gun down and cried for God knows how long. I don't know if you believe in guardian angels or not, but I truly believe mine showed up that night and kept me from pulling that trigger! That little picture I'm talking about is still at my desk some 23 years later. I look at it at some point every single day I'm at work. Sure, most people with offices have pictures of their family somewhere in the office, but now people that know me know the significance of that particular picture. A good friend of mine told me that suicide is a permanent solution to a temporary problem. Please keep that in mind! There is wisdom in that statement.

I learned lots of lessons from the experience of that night. One is, once you're at rock bottom, the only other way is up! Another lesson is that I had my eyes on me. It was a form of selfishness! It's when I got my eyes off me that my life changed for the better. When you are selfish you are headed down a lonely road. You will never find fulfillment, only defeat as I felt that night.

It's amazing when I look back at that time in my life and how stupid my thoughts, ambitions, and actions were. One thing I do know, I'm thankful to this day that I didn't pull that trigger. It easily could have come to an end some 23 years ago. I now look up to God and thank Him for every day I have.

Since then, I've met a wonderful lady, Judy, who became my wife in December of 1993. I was blessed with a daughter through marriage; my two sons have grown and are doing well. My oldest son is married and given us two grandsons. Our daughter is married and has given us a granddaughter. I'm waiting for some news from my youngest son as of this writing.

God doesn't give you the people you want; he gives you the people you need. They might help you, hurt you, leave you, or love you. But no matter what they do, they will make you the person you were meant to be.

Favorite Quotes
Gratefulness Mindsets

❖ "Gratitude helps you to grow and expand; gratitude brings joy and laughter into our life and into the lives of all those around you."-Eileen Cody

❖ "Kindness is a hard thing to give away; it keeps coming back to the giver."-Ralph Scott

❖ "Both in good fiction and in life, you may not always get what you want, but you will probably get what you need. We should be grateful for these things."-Neil Gaiman

❖ "If the only prayer you say in your whole life is 'Thank you' that would suffice."-Meister Echert

❖ "Life is not made up of great sacrifice and duties, but of little things; in which smiles and kindness given habitually are what win and preserve the heart."-Sir Humphrey Davy

❖ It's not happiness that brings us gratitude, it's gratitude that brings us happiness.

❖ "Gratitude is when memory is stored in the heart and not in the mind."-Lionel Hampton

❖ "Nothing is more honorable than a grateful heart." -Seneca

❖ "Feeling gratitude and not expressing it is like wrapping a present and not giving it."-William Arthur Ward

Always remember...
"What you put in your mind is going to come out of you in one form or another. Look what happened with these crazy people who have snapped and killed people in a rampage in shopping malls, movie theaters, and schools. You can only imagine what they were loading into their minds before their actions!"

Roy A. Piercy

CHAPTER 13

Character Traits

Miscellaneous Mindsets

Through the last five years, I wrote down and took notes when I heard good comments, quotes, or thought of something that should be in this book. When I couldn't fit them in the other chapters, I decided to put them in a chapter of their own.

So I hope you enjoy and gain some blessing from them as I have.

- ❖ In your business dealings when you greet others, look them straight in the eye with a firm handshake. My uncle taught me that years ago.

- ❖ Buy great books, even if you don't read every word of them. Your books are a great indication of what your philosophy is. They show what's of interest to you.

❖ Treat everyone you come in contact with the same way you would like to be treated.

❖ Show respect for all law enforcement officers, fire-fighters, veterans, and military personnel. Always remember not to paint law enforcement in a negative way because you saw a few incidents go awry on TV news. Always address a policeman or highway patrolman as officer.

❖ Visit all the great sights this country has to offer. Many are free, so take advantage of that. When you visit a place, be there. You don't need to be using the cell phone, except for pictures.

❖ Show the utmost respect for our American flag. Hundreds of thousands have died for it and our freedoms. The burning of the flag is not free speech. It is utter disrespect and I personally will not have anything to do with anyone who demonstrates in that fashion.

❖ Buy your vegetables and fruit from a farmer who is selling from the back of his truck with a sign he has done himself. You can tell just by talking to him and looking at his hands if he's a farmer.

❖ Be an optimist and not a pessimist. Avoid people who are continually negative. They are a drain and a waste of time.

❖ Never negatively criticize the person who signs your paycheck. If you don't like the one you're working for, find a new job. Remember, change!

❖ Never react when you're angry! The biggest mistakes in life have taken place under these circumstances.

❖ Never measure anyone by their bank account. That's too deceiving. Measure people by their character, by their heart, and how they treat people. You'll know after you've been around them for a while.

❖ Teach your kids the importance of saving and the value of money. Remember that you are their biggest example.

❖ When engaged in conversation and business, never answer your cell phone and allow it to interrupt. It's rude and a terrible habit. Deal with the call later. You're in control, not the caller!

❖ Watch what bridges you burn. You might have to use one to get on the other side of the river someday.

❖ Don't spread yourself too thin! Learn to say no in a polite manner. The greatest mistake I've ever made in the 35 years in my lab business was taking on work I shouldn't have.

❖ Everything comes with a price. Even your freedom isn't free!

❖ When you have a great idea, act on it! You risk the danger of either forgetting about it or someone else coming up with the same idea and succeeding.

❖ Make a bucket list and keep adding to it, for if you do everything on it, you'll have nothing to look forward to.

❖ Never waste an opportunity to tell someone something positive to make them feel good when appropriate.

❖ Always tip a waitress or waiter more than normal on weekends or holidays! Remember that they are sacrificing their time with their families to take care of you!

❖ You don't get a second chance to make a first impression.

❖ After you have worked hard to achieve an important task, reward yourself and enjoy the moment!

❖ Become a great listener and a great reader! Remember great leaders are great readers!

❖ Never reject a breath mint if someone offers you one. They may be politely telling you that you have bad breath!

❖ Time spent with a friend is never wasted time.

❖ Seek and ye shall find, old scripture goes. So whatever you look for in life, if you look hard enough, you will find it. That goes for good and bad. If you look for trouble, you will find it. If you look for great values, wisdom, and great character, you'll find it as well.

❖ Always do the right thing, that's the reputation you want to develop in spite of what others may think.

❖ Do nice things for people. Even people you don't particularly like. They will have a hard time not acting positively.

❖ Doing the right thing isn't always popular. Doing what's popular isn't always the right thing.

❖ Do your best to lift other people up. Putting them down only brings you both down.

❖ When you shake hands on something, treat it as a signed contract.

❖ Happiness doesn't come by accident.

❖ Stop saying "I wish" and start saying "I will".

❖ "Don't sweat the small stuff….. and it's all small stuff!"-Richard Carlson

❖ "We are what we repeatedly do. Excellence then, is not an act, but a habit."-Aristotle

❖ "Two sure ways to fail, think and never do and do and never think."-Zig Ziglar

❖ "The place to improve the world is first in one's own heart, head, and hands. Work outward from there."-Robert Pirsig

❖ "Everything comes with a price, in one form or another!"-Roy Piercy

❖ "Your most important work is always ahead of you, never behind you."-Stephen Covey

❖ "Greatness is not found in possessions, power, position or prestige. It is discovered in goodness, humility, service and character."-William Arthur Ward

Disclosure. . .

I have not been compensated in any way from the people whose books, programs, etc. that I recommend in this book.

That would be a conflict of interest and not fair to you, the reader. The whole purpose is to help you and give you ideas that will make a life-long difference in <u>your</u> life!

Roy A. Piercy

Recommended Reading

Books Every Personal Library Should Have

- ❖ <u>One Thousand Gifts</u>, Ann Voskamp
- ❖ <u>Richest Man in Babylon</u>, *George S. Clason*
- ❖ <u>Double Your Money in America's Finest Companies</u>, *Bill Staton*
- ❖ <u>America's Finest Companies Investment Plan</u>, *Bill Staton*
- ❖ <u>How to Become Financially Free on $50.00 a Month</u>, *Bill and Mary Staton*
- ❖ <u>Total Money Makeover</u>, *Dave Ramsey*
- ❖ <u>Financial Peace University</u>, *Dave Ramsey*
- ❖ <u>Debt Free Living</u>, *Larry Burkett*
- ❖ <u>Finding Financial Freedom</u>, *Grant R. Jeffrey*
- ❖ <u>Creating Wealth</u>, Robert G. Allen

*These recommended books are suggested reading and can be time sensitive. Always seek a professional that you are comfortable with for legal, financial and investment advice.

"It's only when we truly
understand that we have
a limited time on earth,
and we have no way of
knowing when our time
is up, that we will
begin to live each day
to the fullest,
as if it was the
only one we had."

Elizabeth Kubler-Ross
1926 – 2004 age 78
Author of "
Death and Dying"

About the Author

Roy A. Piercy has been a dental technician for 35 years. During that time, through financial experiences, learning from mistakes and hardships, Roy pulled himself out of bankruptcy and spent years of working as hard on himself as he was working on his job in the dental laboratory. Listening and applying all he has learned about the basics of personal finances and personal development from some of the best teachers around, Roy has chosen to share his knowledge and help people (both young and old) that he sees making the same mistakes he used to. It is his mission to help as many people as he can have good foundations and principles that will have a lasting impact on their lives.

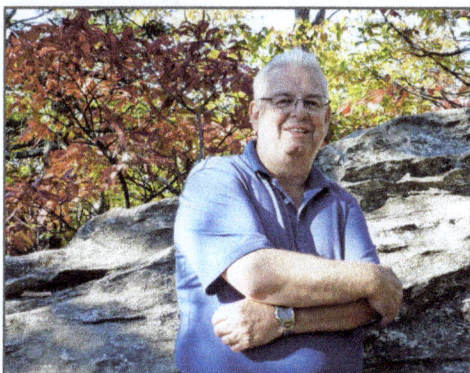

"Although time seems to fly by, it never travels faster than one day at a time. Each day is a new opportunity to live your life to the fullest."

Steve Maraboli
1975-Living
Speaker, Author and
Motivator

www.ingramcontent.com/pod-product-compliance
Lightning Source LLC
Chambersburg PA
CBHW060435090426
42733CB00011B/2283